To: Babs 4-10-08
Happy Birthday
Love,
Cindy

EVERYDAY

Prayers

Spiritual Refreshment for Women

RACHEL QUILLIN

BARBOUR
PUBLISHING

© 2006 by Barbour Publishing, Inc.

ISBN 978-1-59789-068-7

Scripture quotations are taken from the King James Version of the Bible.

Cover design by Kirk DouPonce, dogeareddesign.com

Published by Barbour Publishing, Inc., P.O. Box 719, Uhrichsville, Ohio 44683, www.barbourbooks.com

Our mission is to publish and distribute inspirational products offering exceptional value and biblical encouragement to the masses.

 Member of the
Evangelical Christian
Publishers Association

Printed in China.

5 4 3 2

Contents

*Let us therefore come boldly
unto the throne of grace,
that we may obtain mercy,
and find grace to help in time of need.*

HEBREWS 4:16

What an amazing invitation! We are welcome—any time—to bring any petition before the King of the universe. Not only that, we are also admonished to "come before his presence with thanksgiving" (Psalm 95:2) and "singing" (Psalm 100:2). The all-powerful God we serve is interested in each one of us, and He truly wants to hear what we have to say. That's genuine love!

The words of these prayers are intended to challenge you as you develop a more intimate relationship with your heavenly Father—a relationship He is greatly anticipating.

Anger

If you do not wish to be prone to anger,
do not feed the habit;
give it nothing which may tend to its increase.

EPICTETUS

Controlled Anger

I can't take it, Father.

It sometimes seems like others

deliberately do things to upset me.

Maybe it's just how they are with everyone,

but I have trouble not retaliating.

I try so hard to be like You,

but it's a struggle.

Please help me control my anger;

help me not to be so sensitive.

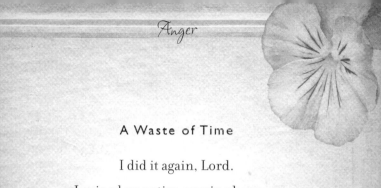

A Waste of Time

I did it again, Lord.

I ruined an entire evening because

of something incredibly ridiculous.

I didn't sleep well because

I was still fuming.

My anger is always such

a waste of time and energy.

Forgive me, Father.

Give me strength to control my temper,

and don't let me ruin any more

evenings for myself or for others.

The Right Time and Place

One of the most interesting stories
in Your Word is about the time
You cleansed the temple.
It has taught me that there is a time
and place for anger.
Sin is always something that
should invoke fury.
Just help me to direct my anger
at the sin and not the sinner.

Reacting Angrily

Father, You know the emotional
roller coaster I've been riding.
I want to be happy for my friends
when they rejoice,
but the pain in my heart is so raw.
It seems like my loved ones
are flaunting their joy,
and I can't help but react angrily.
I know this hurts them
and isn't pleasing to You.
Please help me through this struggle.

Anger Hurts

I was just trying to help.

I knew from personal experience

that he was about to make a mistake.

I tried to be gentle and loving,

but he became so angry,

telling me it was none of my business.

Now he won't even speak to me,

and that hurts.

Please heal the breach, Father.

Children

We can't form our children on our own concepts;
we must take them and love them
as God gives them to us.

JOHANN WOLFGANG VON GOETHE

Reality Parenting

From the time I was a child, one of my

greatest dreams was to be a mother.

I did pretty well when I pretended

with my dolls, but reality is a lot different.

Now that I have children,

I'm not always so sure of myself.

Please, God, give me wisdom

and courage to be a good parent.

Comic Relief

Children can sometimes
be so comical, Lord.
They say the funniest things
or make the silliest faces.
Sometimes all I need to do
on a tough day is watch them.
They'll do something so hilarious
that I can't help but laugh.
I feel better right away.
Children are a wonderful gift.

Children's Games

Lord, my children love it

when I play with them,

and sometimes my participation

in their activities contributes

significantly to their development.

But to be honest,

I'm not very good at their games.

I'm often distracted by

other things I need to do.

Please don't let me lose sight of the truth—

that playing with my children

is an important accomplishment.

God's Truths

There's so much I need to teach

my children about You, Lord.

Throughout their lives

there will be so many questions.

They will face people and situations

that will cause them to doubt You.

Give me opportunities to instill

Your Word so that when doubts come,

they'll stand strong.

A Prayer for My Children

Just the other day someone reminded

me of how important it is

to pray for my children.

So here I am, Lord.

Please protect my kids.

Work in their lives,

so that they will want to serve

You with body, mind, and soul.

Provide those things that they need,

and fill them with contentment

as they bask in the warmth of Your love.

Church

Not until I went into the churches
of America and heard her pulpits flame
with righteousness did I understand
the secret of her genius and power.

ALEXIS DE TOCQUEVILLE

My Church Family

My church is special to me

in so many ways, Lord.

I am so thankful that You have placed me

among such a wonderful group of believers

who encourage me and pray for me.

Allow me to be a blessing to them, as well,

and help me to never forget

how important they are in my life.

Preaching the Truth

Thank You for my pastor, dear God.
He loves You; and he loves those
to whom he ministers.
Knowing that his desire is to present
the truths of the Bible is a great comfort
in a world that is full of false teachings.
Bless my pastor as he continues
to preach Your Word.

Church Decisions

There are many decisions being made

on issues concerning our church, Father.

They aren't easy decisions to make,

and everyone has a different opinion

on what the outcome should be.

Please give us direction and unity.

Work in our midst so that we might

bring others into Your kingdom.

Precious People

There are many precious people
who offer their time and talents
for You, Lord Jesus.
I just want to thank You for each one.
I appreciate those who make a
public contribution as well as those
who work behind the scenes.
They mean more to me than I can say.

The Pastor's Family

I ask You, Lord, to be
with my pastor's family.
He puts in many long hours serving You;
and although he makes a point
to spend time with his wife and children,
they still have to make some sacrifices.
Bless each one of them as they work to bring
Your love to our church and community.

Community

*The life I touch for good or ill will touch
another life, and that in turn, another,
until who knows where the trembling stops
or in what far place my touch will be felt.*

FREDERICK BUECHNER

God-Honoring Activities

There are many ways to be involved

in my community, Father,

and I ask You to show me what to do.

I want to choose the activities that will

help others and that will bring glory to You.

Help me to weigh the possibilities carefully

and to make the best decisions.

Thank You for these opportunities

to honor You.

A Witness in My Community

Lord, there are so many people

in my community who either don't care

about You or who think they will please

You by their own merit;

but several of them don't truly know You.

I ask You to open doors

so I may witness to them.

My prayer is that many will come to You.

Offering Alternatives

I've noticed many disturbing events
in my community, Lord—
activities that in no way glorify You.
I don't become involved,
but some Christians do,
either out of peer pressure or simply
because they don't know it's wrong.
Open their eyes.
Help us band together to offer
Your Light in the darkness.

Newcomers

We live in a

close-knit community, Lord.

In some ways it's nice because

we all stick together.

At the same time,

it can be really hard for newcomers.

Some of us try to welcome them,

but they often move away before long.

Help us, Father, to be more open

to new residents in our town.

A Christian Community

I'm thankful for the Christians

in my town, dear God.

It is such a blessing to fellowship with them.

Recently we've started a Bible study

that is mostly intended

to be an outreach program.

Please let it be successful for Your sake.

Contentment

God is most glorified in us,
when we are most satisfied in Him.

JOHN PIPER

I'm Content

It's a fast-paced world where everyone

wants to get ahead, Father.

Sometimes contentment is frowned upon.

Some folks think of it as laziness

or lack of motivation.

But I know that if I am in the center

of Your will, I'll be content.

That's the only true contentment there is.

Consider the Cat

It doesn't take much to please a kitten,

does it, Lord?

Put him on your lap, rub his head,

and listen to him purr.

What contentment!

I wish I were like that,

but it seems the more I gain,

the more I strive for.

There's not much contentment in that.

Let me learn from the cat

to be satisfied no matter what!

"Poor Me"

Sometimes my attitude is so "poor me"

that I even get sick, Father.

I keep thinking that if only I could

have this or that, life would be easier.

I know I'm missing out on a truly

abundant life by whining so much,

and I ask You to forgive me.

Fill me with contentment.

Labor and Contentment

I am exhausted, Lord,
but I don't think I've ever felt better!
There's nothing quite like
a hard day's work to bring
a tremendous amount of satisfaction.
And I'm really anticipating
the good night's sleep ahead
because I know I pleased You
with my effort today.

"I Will Never Leave Thee"

You've promised to walk with me all the way

and provide all that I need, dear God,

and I'm rejoicing in that guarantee.

What more do I need?

It doesn't matter that the world

presents shiny trinkets.

Their luster dims in the brilliance

of the blessings and contentment

that You give.

Discouragement

Permanence, perseverance,
and persistence in spite of all obstacles,
discouragements, and impossibilities:
It is this, that in all things distinguishes
the strong soul from the weak.

THOMAS CARLYLE

Change of Plans

I feel like crying, Father.

We planned to leave for vacation next week,

but today my husband was a victim of downsizing.

Vacation is now out of the question.

He has to find a new job, or we won't be able

to pay our bills. Help me to remember

that all things work together

for good to those who love You.

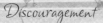

Drenched Spirits

I was staying on top of
my duties for once, Lord.
But then the dryer quit working,
and I still had piles of laundry to finish.
It was fun hanging the clothes out to dry
and pretending I was a pioneer—
until the rains came.
The clothes were drenched,
and so were my spirits.
I wanted to give up.
Please remind me that
You are with me through the storms.

Don't Quit

Lord, I don't want to be a quitter;

but I've tried so hard to be like You,

and I keep messing up.

I know You said that with You

all things are possible,

and I need to be reminded of that daily.

Don't let me give up.

Help me to remember that

You aren't finished with me yet.

Count It All as Joy

It's hard to see discouragement
as a blessing, Lord.
But You said we should count it as a joy.
The trials will increase my patience
and mold me into a more mature believer.
When I look at it that way,
it's much easier to thank You
for the difficult times.

34

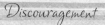

Encouraging Others

You gave me an amazing
opportunity today, Father,
and it's all a result of
a discouraging situation.
You helped me as I struggled
through the problem,
and because of that I was able
to encourage someone else
who faced a similar difficulty.
You really are an awesome God!

Family

*The happiest moments of my life
have been the few which I have passed
at home in the bosom of my family.*

THOMAS JEFFERSON

Family Blessings

Among Your many blessings,

my family ranks near the top.

They share my joys and help

bear my burdens. Dear Jesus,

I know that You selected each of my relatives

to be a part of my life in a special way,

and I thank You for each of them.

May I bring happiness to them

in some way, too!

Godly Parents

Dear Lord, I got my first glimpse of You

through the lives of my parents.

What a blessing to have two such godly

people as an intimate part of my

childhood and early adult years.

Thank You that they cared enough

to instill godly principles in me and loved

me enough to introduce me to You.

Family Reunions

We had a family reunion the other day,

and I was surprised at how much

our family has grown.

I used to never really enjoy these gatherings,

but this time was different.

It was a reminder of the great blessing

You've bestowed on me.

I realized, also, the opportunity

I had to present a testimony of

Your love to those who'd never heard.

I guess reunions aren't so bad after all.

Facing Differences

Lord, as large as my family is,

there are bound to be some members

whose life views are significantly

different than mine.

At times this gets annoying,

particularly when they attempt

to force their outlook on me.

Give me the strength to stand for what

I know to be true, and help me to love

my family despite our differences.

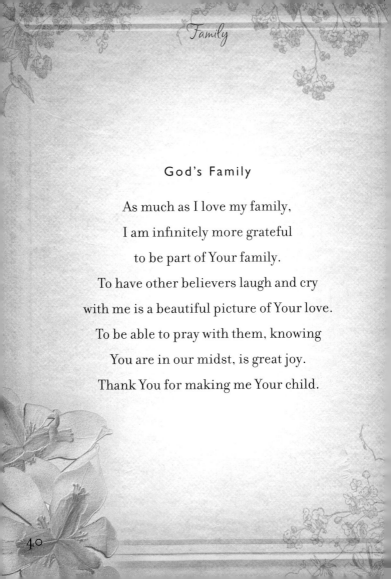

God's Family

As much as I love my family,
I am infinitely more grateful
to be part of Your family.
To have other believers laugh and cry
with me is a beautiful picture of Your love.
To be able to pray with them, knowing
You are in our midst, is great joy.
Thank You for making me Your child.

Fear

Inaction breeds doubt and fear.
Action breeds confidence and courage.
If you want to conquer fear,
do not sit home and think about it.
Go out and get busy.

DALE CARNEGIE

Peace in the Midst of Terror

Lord, when I think about the world
in which I'm raising my children,
I tremble. Crime, hatred, terrorism—
they're everywhere, and they scare me.
I know I should remember that You
are in control, and I try, but sometimes
I get too caught up in what's happening.
Please forgive me, and give me peace.

Fear of the Unknown

I have to laugh when I consider

the silly childhood fears I had—

mostly fears of the unknown.

But when I consider the truth,

even now my fears are mostly

still of the unknown.

It's not so silly now, though,

because I should be trusting You

instead of worrying.

Please help my thoughts to be on You.

Wise Fear

"The fear of the LORD is
the beginning of wisdom" (Psalm 111:10).
Sometimes this passage from Your Word
seems almost contradictory, Lord.
But there is healthy fear,
and then there's crippling fear.
I know this passage means that my respect
of You is so deep that I abhor sin.
Please help me to have this wise fear.

The Color Yellow

One of the cutest songs I know
is about a child peering into a box of crayons
and comparing the colors to the Christian life.
Yellow represents the cowardly believer—
one who is afraid to share
Christ's love with others.
Please don't let me be yellow.
Let me be courageous for You!

Afraid to Surrender

Why are people afraid to surrender
their lives to You, Lord?
I know some are fearful
that You will ask something of them
that they can't bear.
Can't they understand that You'll
strengthen them through every task?
Don't they realize the joy they're missing?
God, break down the barriers
that hinder Your work.

Finances

The real measure of our wealth
is how much we'd be worth
if we lost everything.

J. H. JOWETT

———

Managing Money

It's funny, Lord.

It seems like I always wish I had more money,

but dealing with it can sometimes be a pain.

Keeping it organized, making sure my bills

are paid—at times it's overwhelming.

Please give me a clear mind and wisdom

to handle my financial responsibilities

according to Your will.

My Rich Father

Sometimes I find myself worrying

about my financial situation.

I have a tendency to forget that my Father

owns the cattle on a thousand hills—

and everything else, too.

I know You'll take care of me.

Although I might not fully understand

wealth in this life,

I have amazing riches to anticipate.

What a thrill that is!

Healthy Attitudes

So often, Lord,
I see relationships crumbling,
and much of the time a money issue
is what starts the process.
Some people are careless or dishonest
in their spending;
others just want too much.
As a result there is a lot of
bitterness and hatred.
Please help me to have a proper
outlook when money is involved.

The Widow's Mites

Lately there have been times
when it's been a little hard to tithe.
We have trouble paying our bills,
so we do without things.
The worst thing, though, is thinking
about how little our meager
contribution actually benefits. Lord,
I've been trying to remember
the widow's mites, and that does help.
Let me take courage from her example.

Extras

Dear God, I am so thankful that You

have provided for me.

Sometimes that blessing even goes

above and beyond my needs.

I now ask for wisdom in handling these gifts.

My desire is to glorify You and to make sure

that I'm not controlled by money.

Please help me use it in a way

that honors You.

Forgiveness

Forgiveness needs to be accepted,
as well as offered,
before it is complete.

C. S. LEWIS

Opportunities to Forgive

Growing up with ornery siblings,

I had plenty of chances

to practice forgiveness.

I guess that's good because

I still have opportunities to forgive.

Sometimes it isn't easy,

but it feels so much better to let go

of the hurt than to hold a grudge.

Thank You for giving me these occasions.

Christ Understands

Lord, You've been through things
that I will never experience,
so You understand how hard it is to forgive.
Even though You've experienced
the worst insult, You never put me down
for thinking that the wrong
done to me is unbearable.
Instead, You just give me strength
to do what is necessary.
How can I thank You?

A Friend's Forgiveness

I can't believe it, Father.
I really messed up this time,
and my friend still forgave me.
I didn't really expect her to
ever want to speak to me again,
but she hugged me and told me
we'd just start again.
That felt so wonderful!
Thank You for friends who forgive.

Natural Consequences

Dear Lord, I know You've forgiven
me for that horrible wrong.
I thought when I repented
that would take care of things,
but I'm learning that the natural
consequences still hurt.
I know they won't disappear,
but I pray that You will use them in
a positive way—perhaps to keep others
from making the same mistake.

Seventy Times Seven

Seventy times seven.
Wow! That's an enormous
amount of forgiveness, Lord.
Looking at it from one perspective
it seems outrageous; but
from the other side of the spectrum,
I hope someone would do it for me.
That's one of the nicest things about
forgiveness in the human realm—it's
"give and receive."

Friends

True happiness consists not
in the multitude of friends,
but in their worth and choice.

SAMUEL JOHNSTON

~~~

Finding Friends

Father, choosing friends isn't always easy.

I want to find individuals who share

my values and my love for You.

There just doesn't seem to be

an abundance of people around

who care about You.

Please lead me to the places where

I'll be able to find companions

who will glorify You.

Lord, Carry My Friend

My friend is hurting, dear Jesus.

She's had so many struggles

in her life lately, and she feels like

she's about to hit rock bottom.

I've tried to be there for her, but

right now she needs You in a special way.

Please let her know that You want

to carry her through this trial.

Help her to trust You.

My Best Friend

I think my best friend is a lot like You, Lord.

She offers me spiritual encouragement;

she's there for me in the happy times and

the sad; and she'd do anything for me.

How could I not love her?

People of her nature are like precious pearls.

I'm so blessed to have her in my life!

David and Jonathan

I've been reading about
Jonathan and David, Father.
What an incredible pair of friends.
Jonathan's willingness to take risks
on David's behalf is unbelievable,
especially considering that he knew
David would be king in his place.
Lord, that's the kind of friend I want to be.

Unequally Yoked

I guess I've always wanted to give
people the benefit of the doubt,
but I haven't always been careful enough.
I've ended up becoming too close to
people who disregard You,
and sometimes their influence
on me has been too great.
Father, please help me be friendly
but not intimate with unbelievers.

Goals

I know the price of success: dedication,
hard work, and an unremitting devotion
to the things you want to see happen.

Frank Lloyd Wright

———— ✦ ————

Reached Goals

Sometimes I get a little discouraged, Jesus.
I feel like I've reached all the goals I've set
for myself and that there's nothing for me
to achieve that would bring any excitement.
Please give me a new outlook. Give me
wisdom as I set new goals, and help me
to give You the glory when I succeed.

To-Do Lists

I didn't really think

my goals were far-fetched.

My "to-do" list only had three major tasks,

yet I barely made it through two.

It seems I've worked all day

and accomplished nothing.

I feel disgusted with myself,

but tomorrow's another day, Lord.

Give me the right attitude as I begin again.

Consulting Christ

Lord, often in my daily planning
I forget to consult You.
Then I wonder why things don't work
out the way I think they should.
Forgive my arrogant attitude.
I know that only as You guide
me through the day
will I find joy in accomplishments.
Show me how to align my goals
with Your will.

Blank Stares

Today I'm struggling, Jesus.

I have a specific goal that needs to be met,

but it requires clarity of mind.

The project is spread out before me,

but I'm staring at it blankly.

I know You want me to work on it,

and I need Your guidance.

Give me the ability to think

and complete the task.

Thank You for Goals

Thank You for goals, Lord.
Although they require work,
they give me something to look forward to.
The effort put forth is exhilarating, and
the sense of accomplishment rewarding.
You make me a stronger person
just by giving me work to do.

Godly Character

*The Christian idea has not
been tried and found wanting.
It has been found difficult and left untried.*

G. K. CHESTERTON

Reality Strikes

Dear God, sometimes godly character

sounds so easy to attain when

I'm sitting in church,

listening to the pastor speak.

In my heart I know I want it;

in my mind I believe it's possible.

Making the ideal become reality is

much harder. I need Your strength.

Please help me develop godly character.

Godly Examples

I've seen quite a few examples
of godly people, and I'm so thankful
You've allowed them to cross my path,
Father. It's a real encouragement to see
other people who are becoming
more and more like You.
It helps me in my own quest
for Christlikeness.
Thank You for bringing
these individuals into my life.

Special Instructions

Thank You for Your Word, Father.
Without it I would be a helpless cause
in regard to developing godly character.
I'm so glad You preserved these
special words that give me specific
instruction on how to live.
Help me to hide these scriptures
in my heart so that I'm able to rely
on them throughout my life.

Being Godly on Purpose

Lord, I was recently reminded that
godly character doesn't just happen.
I have to purpose in my heart
to live a life pleasing to You.
Only then will I be able to stand strong
when peer pressure threatens to undo me.
I want to commit daily to obeying You.

Awake to Righteousness

You are far from silent about how
You expect me to live, dear God.
You've commanded me to be like You,
and that includes righteous living.
You've explicitly said,
"Awake to righteousness, and sin not"
(1 Corinthians 15:34).
I don't know if the message
could be any more plain.
I must be righteous!

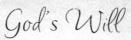

God's Will

*I find that doing God's will leaves me
no time for disputing about His plans.*

GEORGE MACDONALD

The Center of God's Will

Lord, I know that in the center of

Your will are peace, joy,

and many other rich blessings.

I'd like to experience all these things,

but the trouble I seem to have is

figuring out what Your will is for me.

Please help me be attentive when You speak,

and give me a heart willing to be used by You.

Specifics in God's Word

Sometimes I get so frustrated, Lord.

I've asked what You want from me,

but it seems You've remained silent.

Then I realize that there are specifics in Your

Word that I should automatically be doing.

I haven't always been obedient to those,

so how can I expect to know more?

Forgive me, Father. I want to obey.

The Bigger Picture

There have been some things happening
lately that I just don't understand, Lord.
I know You see the bigger picture and
that all that happens is part of Your plan,
but sometimes I need a reminder.
Help me focus on the promise
that all things work together
for good to those who love You.

God's Will for Loved Ones

I've spent a lot of time praying
about Your will in my life, Lord,
but I have many loved ones who also
need to know the work You have for them.
Help them to be open to Your leading,
and give me grace to accept what You
call them to—even if it's not
what I had in mind.

God Won't Force It

Your desire is that we seek and do Your will,

dear God, but You'll never force us to do it.

You've laid unique paths before each of us,

and it's because You love us all in a special way.

Help us not to envy Your plans for others;

let us complete our work with joy.

Grief

If we had no winter,
the spring would not be so pleasant;
if we did not sometimes taste of adversity,
prosperity would not be so welcome.

ANNE BRADSTREET

Deep Sorrow

I know You understand grief

better than anyone else, Father,

but right now I feel as if no one

has traveled this road before.

My sorrow is so deep, my pain so intense.

It seems I'm all alone. I need You, God.

My soul cries out for relief.

Please heal my broken heart,

and help me smile once more.

Loss of a Pet

My child's dog died this morning, Lord,

and he is full of sorrow.

Some mock his tears,

but his grief is very real to him.

I hug him close and offer words of comfort,

but that won't bring back his playmate.

Please fill the void in his life,

and comfort him in Your special way.

God's Comfort

Dear Jesus, my sister is grieving

for her son who rejects You.

My friend is losing her father

to a dreadful illness.

My neighbor's marriage is crumbling

despite her best efforts to pull it together.

They need Your comfort.

They, and so many like them.

Soothe their heartaches, Father.

Freedom to Grieve

It's so hard to express grief
in our society, Jesus,
but I'm glad You don't reject us when we do.
After all, You grieved,
and You showed me how to handle perhaps
one of the deepest human emotions.
Thank You for letting me come to You
when I'm hurting.
Thank You for Your love.

Yes, God Loves Me

I've been concentrating so much
on my grief, Lord,
that I'm afraid my perspective of
You has become warped.
I wonder why You allow bad things
to happen, and sometimes I even question
whether or not You really love me.
I know the truth is that You are right
there with me, wanting me to
trust and love You more.
Help me keep that in focus.

Happiness

*It's not how much we have, but how much
we enjoy, that makes happiness.*

CHARLES SPURGEON

Those Happy Times

A lot of times I've heard people say
that Christians can be joyful without
being happy, and I know that's true.
Still, I relish those happy times in life
It feels good to laugh so hard
that I'm crying and to smile
because I see something cute.
Thank You for giving me
happy times to enjoy, dear Jesus.

Bearable Burdens

Lord, we sometimes sing a song

about being happy because

You took our burdens all away.

I guess You really just make

the burdens more bearable.

Still, that's something great to sing about,

and it does bring happiness.

I'm so glad You're there

to lighten the load.

Simple Blessings

Thank You for the many happy times
You've given me.
So often it's the little things in life—
the first robin in the spring,
the first homegrown tomato of the season,
even a brilliant sunset.
These simple blessings evoke
the biggest smiles
and make me the happiest!

Bad Happiness

I'm embarrassed, Lord,

and I need Your cleansing.

Someone at church has been

giving me trouble for a while.

I just discovered that something

unfortunate happened to him, and I gloated.

I tried to keep my happiness under cover,

but it was there, and it shouldn't have been.

Please don't let me rejoice

at others' misfortunes.

The Source of Happiness

I'm glad money isn't required

to obtain true happiness,

or I wouldn't get much.

You meet my needs sufficiently,

but the happiness I enjoy when I'm

with family or just relaxing

with a good book on a lazy afternoon

is beyond sufficient.

True happiness really can't

be bought, can it, Jesus?

It all comes from You.

Health

If taking vitamins doesn't keep
you healthy enough, try more laughter:
The most wasted of all days is that
on which one has not laughed.

NICOLAS-SEBASTIEN CHAMFORT

What's Right?

Sometimes I get pretty confused, Lord.

I try to eat right, exercise properly,

and get plenty of rest,

but all of the "experts" say different

things about what I should be doing.

It's important that I am a good steward

of the body You've given me,

so please help me to care

for myself the right way.

Enjoying Good Health

I thank You, Father,

for giving me good health.

There are so many who

do not enjoy this blessing.

Sometimes I'm tempted to complain

about the aches and pains that

we all face from time to time,

but I really have no reason to.

You have been good to me.

Sufficient Grace

I've been facing a physical difficulty lately,
and it seems to be getting worse.
I've prayed, dear God. Oh, how I've prayed.
Sometimes it feels like You are so far away,
but I know You are right here next to me
offering Your sufficient grace and strength.
Help me to accept this as Your answer.

Sick Children

Dear Lord, all the kids are sick,

and I am at my wit's end.

They don't understand

why they're miserable.

All I can do is hold them close

and let them know I love them,

but sometimes I wonder if it's enough.

I ask You to heal them.

Please help me be the mother they need.

Christ Still Heals

You brought healing to
so many people in the Bible, Jesus.
Those were exciting times
for those individuals,
and it's still a spectacular miracle
when You make someone whole today.
Thank You for the many times
You've touched my sick body
or brought relief to my loved ones.
Your loving touch produces great joy.

Home

Mid pleasures and palaces, though we may roam,
Be it ever so humble, there's no place like home.

JOHN HOWARD PAYNE

Filled with Love

Lord, let my home be a comforting

haven for my family and friends.

May it be a place where they

can momentarily escape

the pressures of this world.

Help me to do my best to make

it a place where people will know

they are loved by me and,

more importantly, by You.

Where the Heart Is

I've heard it said that

home is where the heart is,

and I suppose there's a lot of truth in that.

My home is such a special place,

and it seems that often

when I'm somewhere else,

I am longing to be back in that place,

surrounded by what is

comfortable and familiar.

Thank You for that opportunity

to return home.

Welcome to My Home

Do You feel welcome in my home,
Father? Are You happy to be here,
or are You ashamed to call me Your child?
I want You to be more important
in our daily lives than anything else,
and I want to open our home to You
to use in any way You choose.

The Real Me

It's not that I mean to be two-faced,

Lord, but I guess I'm just more

comfortable at home.

I'm not as careful about what I say,

and often my weaknesses seem exaggerated

because I'm not always on guard.

That's how I end up hurting

those I love the most.

Father, please let the "real me"

be Christlike at home—and away.

Family Time

Thank You for my home, dear Jesus.

I just love to be here.

I can't explain the joy that comes

from being surrounded by those I love.

Whether our home is filled with laughter

during game night or shrouded

in silent contemplation during family

devotions, I can feel Your presence,

and I am uplifted.

Humility

God created the world out of nothing,
and so long as we are nothing,
He can make something out of us.

Martin Luther

————

Unnatural Humility

We're by nature very proud, Jesus.

Humility certainly doesn't come easily.

But You are humble, and You are the

example I am to follow regardless

of what comes readily.

Teach me to be more like You.

Teach me to be a servant.

To Be Like Jesus

Father, I was amazed to see
a very attractive, well-dressed lady
go out of her way to help an individual
of completely opposite description.
The dirt and smell didn't seem
to bother her, and the heartfelt hug
so brightened the other
person's countenance.
I thought how like You the lady was—
how like You I want to be.

Behind the Scenes

There are so many people who desire
those high-profile positions,
and there's nothing wrong with that;
but I want to thank You for those
people who are cheerfully willing
to take the less noticeable jobs.
Their humble contributions
help things run more smoothly,
and that's how I want to be—willing
to do whatever needs to be done.

Humiliating Lessons

A promotion opportunity came up at work,

and I felt like I met the qualifications.

I was sure I would get the job,

but an outsider was hired instead.

That stung! I guess if I had learned

to be humble in the first place,

it might not have hurt so badly.

Let me learn from this, Jesus.

Resolving Arguments

I overheard an argument and witnessed
a display of true humility, Lord.
One individual had a legitimate gripe,
yet he backed down from the other
person just to resolve the quarrel.
He obviously wasn't afraid
of the other person;
he just wanted the friendship restored.
That's how You want us to react, isn't it?

Joy

The joy of the Lord will arm us against
the assaults of our spiritual enemies
and put our mouths out of taste for those
pleasures with which the tempter baits his hooks.

MATTHEW HENRY

A New Song

Since You came into my life, dear Jesus,

I am filled with a fascinating joy.

You've given me a new song, and I find

myself singing it at the most unusual times.

Sometimes I receive questioning looks,

but it gives me an opportunity to share

with others what You've done in my life.

I pray they seek Your joy, too.

Songs of Joy

I love listening to children
singing songs about joy.
They're such positive tunes,
and I find myself wanting to join in.
And why shouldn't I?
I'm sure it would please You
to hear adults belting out these joyful
Sunday school verses with as much
conviction as the little ones.
After all, You've given us our joy.

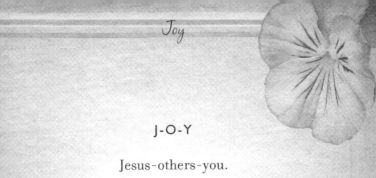

J-O-Y

Jesus-others-you.
What a simple yet profound
definition of joy.
And I'm beginning to see
just how much this really works.
I guess that's because when
You are first in my life,
everything else is properly prioritized.
Although putting others before
myself isn't always easy,
it feels wonderful when I do it.

Joyful Knowledge

Although the world might not
think that my circumstances
always warrant a song,
I am rejoicing in the knowledge
of what lies ahead.
I have perfect hope
of an eternity with You.
I have joy in the belief that You
are with me each step of the way.
You have put a smile in my heart.
Thank You, Lord.

Tidings of Joy

You brought joy to Abraham and Sarah

when You said they'd have a son.

In a similar way, Mary rejoiced.

And the many times You announced,

"Thy faith hath saved thee,"

brought forth smiles.

Your Word still has that effect today.

Thank You for giving us joy!

Life's Challenges

*Many men owe the grandeur of their lives
to their tremendous difficulties.*

CHARLES H. SPURGEON

A New Challenge Each Day

Oh, how I enjoy a good challenge, Lord;

and each day challenges me anew!

Thank You for these opportunities—

for each exciting adventure.

My desire is that I might face each task

in a godly manner and that I might

honor You in all I say and do.

Joy in the Challenge

Father, I thought challenges were

supposed to be positive motivation,

but when I woke up this morning,

I'm afraid my outlook

wasn't very optimistic.

All I could think about were the

myriad mundane jobs I had to do.

Forgive me.

Help me to accept each challenge with joy.

Godly Patience

I have to admit that one
of the greatest challenges I face
each day is the need for patience.
I'm tested regularly on the subject,
and too often I fail. Lord,
I know I won't win this battle overnight,
but with Your help,
I'll daily work toward
achieving godly patience.

A Definition

Life's challenge—how can I describe it?
I might say it is my best-laid plans
peppered with interruptions,
broken equipment, lack of sleep,
and the necessity to complete a task
in the allotted amount of time
regardless of the circumstances.
It sounds rough,
and it often seems that way,
but with Your help I can endure!

Joshua's Example

Joshua faced a tough challenge,
didn't he, Lord?
He had to get a rather difficult
group of people across a huge river
right at flood stage,
and that was merely the beginning.
But he didn't flinch.
He trusted Your promises
to be with him, and I can, too.
Thank You for reminding me
of Joshua's example
right when I needed it most.

Loneliness

An infinite God can give all of Himself to each of His children. He does not distribute Himself that each may have a part, but to each one He gives all of Himself as fully as if there were no others.

A. W. TOZER

Monday Holidays

I used to love Monday holidays, Lord.

The long weekends, the picnics,

and family fun—I have great memories.

But now it's different. I live too far away to go home.

My friends are with their families,

and I don't want to intrude.

But I'm lonely. Please ease that emptiness, and

help me reach out to others in similar situations.

Christ's Loneliness

Lord, how alone You must have been
in the garden when the disciples fell asleep.
And when God turned His back as
You hung on the cross—was there
anything to compare to what You felt?
Yet You did it willingly.
You understand when I'm lonely,
and I thank You for being there
during those times.

A Lonely World

It can be a lonely world at times—
especially when people don't
understand why I choose to serve You.
I guess it kind of makes me
homesick for heaven.
I can't wait to be with You
forever and to spend time with others
who are praising You, too!

Reaching Out

Dear God, I was just noticing

all the people around me who

really could use a friend.

For whatever reason,

they're alone and hurting.

I need to reach out to them.

I ask You to give me opportunities

and ideas to let them know I care.

Let me make the world

a little friendlier for them.

The Right Solution

Father, a friend of mine got tired

of being the only "single" around.

We tried to ease the loneliness,

but she felt that marriage

was the only answer.

She fell for the first guy

who showed interest,

and now she's even more miserable.

Please give her strength,

and help others learn from her mistake.

Love

The best portion of a good man's life,
His little, nameless, unremembered acts,
of kindness and of love.

WILLIAM WORDSWORTH

True Love

Love—what a beautiful word!

Yet many people are so cynical about it,

dear Jesus. I guess that's because there is

so much artificial affection in this world,

but I'd like for people to see true love—

Your love—in my life.

Please give me the ability

to love as You do.

Loving God

I say I love You, Father, although
I'm not sure it goes as deep as it should.
I want it to, though.
I want to be so in love with You
that it shows in every aspect of my life.
Help me to develop the intimacy
with You that I should have.

I Love You

Today my little girl turned her

cherubic face toward me and said

so sincerely, "I love you."

She doesn't fully understand,

but she means it as best as she knows how.

Just to hear those precious words

in her sweet little voice brightened my day,

and I thank You for that blessing.

Love and Fear

Looking at it from a human perspective,

it doesn't seem like love and fear

are remotely connected.

Yet we are admonished many times

to love and fear You.

It's a little hard to comprehend,

but when we really consider who You are

and what You've done for us,

how can we not both fear and love You?

No Excuses

I want to say,

"You don't know what that person's like.

He's impossible to love!"

But You told me to love my enemies.

You showed me how to do this

by dying for me even when my life

was loathsome from sin.

I was hideous, unlovable, but You still cared.

I have no excuse not to love my enemies.

Missions

The history of missions is the
history of answered prayer.

SAMUEL ZWERNER

Provision for Missions

In Your Word, You've commanded us
to take the gospel to all nations.
You've also said that when we're
obedient, You'll meet our needs.
Please meet the needs
of our missionaries, Lord.
Provide what they need physically
and spiritually, and let many souls
be saved as a result.

World Missions and Me

Father, I believe the mission field

You have for me is right here at home,

but I know You want me to be involved

in world missions, as well.

Help me to faithfully pray

for our missionaries.

Give me wisdom as to how You

would have me financially support them,

and show me any other way I can help them.

In Harm's Way

Dear God, so many missionaries
are in harm's way.
They face terrorist threats,
unsanitary living conditions,
and even dangerous animals or
illnesses that I can't begin to fathom.
Please protect them, Father.
They've willingly taken these risks
so that others might know Your love.
Keep them under Your wing of safety.

Now Entering the Mission Field

There is a sign over the door
at church that states:
"You Are Now Entering the Mission Field."
You called it harvest, Lord, and You want
me to do my part in gathering.
Lead me to souls who
are prepared for the gospel.
Let me be alert to opportunities
to witness for You.

124

Those Left Behind

Father, I'd like to take just
a moment to pray for the extended
families of missionaries.
We often forget that
as obedient servants take
Your gospel abroad,
their relatives are left behind.
The separation can be difficult.
Ease the loneliness.
Bless each family member in a special way.

Modesty

Modesty is to merit,
what shade is to figures in a picture;
it gives strength and makes it stand out.

JEAN DE LA BRUYERE

An Immodest World

Your Word clearly demands

modesty of Your children,

God, but to be honest,

it's hard in this world.

It's difficult to even find apparel that

would fit Your definition of modesty,

and the attitudes of people

are even more indecent.

I need Your strength to obey

even when it's not easy.

126

Modest Example

So many people think that modesty

is only a clothing issue, but

You've shown me that it's so much more.

It's an attitude akin to humility,

and it's what You want from me.

Even in this You set

the example for me, Jesus.

Help me to follow the pattern

You've given me.

My Heavenly Mansion

Enormous homes seem to be what
are expected in this "get more" society.
Calling someone's home "modest"
is almost derogatory, and that's a shame.
Help me not to envy those who have more.
My home meets my needs and gives
me something to look forward to
as I anticipate my heavenly mansion.

Praise Be to God

I guess we all like to receive

praise from time to time, and

in moderation it's probably good for us.

But, Father, give me a modest heart

about the honor when it does come.

Don't let me become puffed with pride.

I want to give the glory to You,

for without You I am nothing.

Don't Strut Your Stuff

You've allowed me to excel
at some things, dear God,
and I'm glad to be of use to You.
But there have been times
I've been a little embarrassed
because others want me to flaunt
my accomplishments.
I know sometimes sharing what
I've done will benefit others,
but help me to distinguish
between helpfulness and bragging.

Neighbors

Intercessory prayer might be defined
as loving our neighbor on our knees.

CHARLES BRENT

The Folks Next Door

I didn't have many neighbors growing up,

and I'd heard a lot of horror stories about

neighbors in general.

When I moved into my own home,

I was more than a little leery

about the folks next door.

It didn't take long to realize

what a blessing they are.

I only pray that I'll be

a good neighbor in return.

That Important First Step

Lord, my neighbors are some of

the most rude and inconsiderate

people I've ever known.

It's hard not to complain about them,

but I don't have a right to.

They aren't Christians,

and I've never witnessed to them.

Why would they act differently?

Forgive me, Father.

I will take them Your Word.

Please open their hearts.

Who Is My Neighbor?

One young man asked You
who his neighbor was,
and You told him the story
of the good Samaritan.
I've always admired the Samaritan,
but I sometimes find I'm more
like the priest or Levite,
finding reasons not to help others
How this must hurt You!
Cleanse me, Lord.
Mold me into a good neighbor.

Weekday Christians

There's a lot of importance to be placed

on making sure we're godly, not only

on Sunday but throughout the week.

After all, that's mostly

when our neighbors see us.

I'm so grateful for godly neighbors

who live their faith on a daily basis, Lord.

Their influence on me is profound.

Neighborly Influence

I'm a little concerned about

the effect some of my neighbors might

be having upon my children, Lord.

I've tried to bring them up

according to Your Word,

but peer pressure can be quite strong.

Please help them to be faithful

and to stay on the right path.

Our Country and Leaders

*Providence has given to our people
the choice of their rulers, and it is the duty,
as well as the privilege and interest of
our Christian nation to select
and prefer Christians for their rulers.*

JOHN JAY

Our Freedom

It brings tears to my eyes just to hear

"The Star-Spangled Banner,"

and I get choked up when I see

veterans being honored.

I know it's because of the sacrifices

made by others that I have freedom

to worship You as I choose.

Thank You for my country.

May I never take these liberties for granted.

One Nation Under God

Dear God, I am so weary of
the bickering in our nation.
It disturbs me to see people attempting
to remove You from schools, courtrooms,
and anywhere else they think of.
They distort history and deny that
this nation was founded
with You as her leader.
Heal us, Lord.
Help us return to You!

Righteous Leaders

You've said that righteous leaders
result in rejoicing among the people,
and You've given us the opportunity
to choose our leaders.
With this privilege,
You've given us the responsibility
of electing godly people.
Father, give us wisdom to recognize
these individuals and to put
them into office.

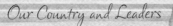

Righteousness Exalteth a Nation

I love the Proverbs, Lord,
and one of my favorites says,
"Righteousness exalteth a nation."
(Proverbs 14:34).
For many years our country
has been powerful among her peers,
and it's because You were part
of the lives of the people.
We've begun to abandon You, though.
Please forgive us, and restore us
to a right relationship with You.

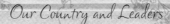

On Behalf of Our Soldiers

There is a very special group

of Americans whom I'd like

to bring before You, Father.

They are our servicemen and -women.

So many of them are in harm's way, Lord.

They need Your protection in a way

I cannot even comprehend.

Please put a hedge around them.

Bring them safely home.

Peace

*A great many people are trying to make peace,
but that has already been done.
God has not left it for us to do;
all we have to do is enter into it.*

D. L. MOODY

Gentle Peace

Thank You, Lord, for this opportunity

to bask in the peace that You offer.

As I sit here in the woods, listening to

the creek gently bubbling over the stones,

I am reminded how Your presence in my

life soothes even in the midst of chaos.

I'm glad I have Your peace!

The Gift of Peace

Father, as I look around,

I see so much turmoil.

My heart breaks as I watch

the trials people attempt to face

without You in their lives.

They don't realize the perfect peace

that You want to give them,

and many of them don't

want to hear about it.

Speak to their hearts.

Help them accept Your gift.

Peaceful Rest

How beautiful to watch a sleeping child!

With his arm wrapped gently around

his teddy bear and his thumb in his mouth,

he embodies peacefulness.

As I watch him, I am reminded that You've

promised peaceful rest to those in Your care.

Oh, how I thank You for this!

Butter-Tub Ships

Last week was pretty hectic, dear Jesus,

but I was reminded that

You hadn't forgotten me.

My daughter came home with a butter tub

that had been converted into a ship.

It was accompanied by a picture

of You calming the storm.

Across the top were emblazoned the words,

"Peace be still."

At Peace with Others

There are a lot of people
with whom I must get along.
We come from a variety of backgrounds,
and we don't always agree on everything.
I've found, however, that peaceful
disagreement makes for better
relationships, so help me to do my part
to live peaceably with others.

Prayers of Praise

Praise God, from Whom all blessings flow;
Praise Him, all creatures here below;
Praise Him above, ye heav'nly host;
Praise Father, Son, and Holy Ghost.

THOMAS KEN, "DOXOLOGY"

Evening Rainbows

When I first caught a glimpse

of that rainbow, I was thrilled.

When I really stopped to look

at its brilliance, I was awed.

Only You could have painted something

so glorious across the expanse

of the evening sky.

Thank You for the beauty of Your promises.

All Creation Speaks

We've traveled through several states

recently and seen many scenic pictures.

Golden fields, purple mountains,

sparkling lakes. . . How could anyone believe

that something so amazing just happened?

Your awesome creation speaks the truth,

and to You belongs all the glory!

Matchless Grace

The song talks of praising You

for Your matchless grace,

and how could I go through

a single day without doing so?

I don't understand why

You love and forgive me,

but I wish to offer my sincerest thanks

for these bountiful gifts.

You are a wonderful Savior!

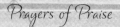
For Each New Day

Every day there is something for which
I can offer You praise, dear God!
To begin with, we have
the promise of a fresh start—
a new opportunity to serve You.
Throughout the day
You show Your majesty
in a multitude of ways.
You are an awesome God!

Sacrifice of Praise

Lord, may the life I live be a continual

sacrifice of praise to You.

You, who have done so much for me,

ask only that I give my life wholly to You.

How can I refuse?

Let what others see in me be cause

for them to glorify You, too.

Prayers of Thanks

Best of all is it to preserve everything in a pure,
still heart, and let there be for every pulse
a thanksgiving, and for every breath a song.

KONRAD VON GESNER

New Compassions

I really didn't want to get up this morning, Father.

My blankets seemed like good

protection from the cares of the day.

But when I saw the glorious sunrise

and heard the cheerful, singing birds,

I was reminded that Your compassions

are new every morning.

I knew everything would be fine.

Thank You for Your faithfulness.

God's in Control

Thank You, Lord, that You have
a perfect plan for my life.
I know I don't always understand it,
but You know what's best,
and everything that happens is for a
reason—that You might be glorified.
I'm so glad that You are in control
and that I need not worry.

Summer Rains

That refreshing rain!

Oh, how badly we needed it.

The fields were parched

and the rivers drying,

Just when we thought we could

take no more of the heat,

You sent the cool, cleansing rains.

Now the garden's growing,

the streams flowing,

and our hearts are offering thanks!

O Give Thanks unto the Lord

Father, I was working on a series of lessons

for the children's Sunday school,

and I felt led to concentrate

on the verse that says,

"O give thanks unto the LORD" (Psalm 136:1).

I realized how many things

we have to be thankful for

and how many lessons

in Your Word back this up.

You are indeed worthy of our thanks!

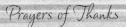

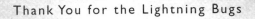

Thank You for the Lightning Bugs

I am convinced, Father,

that one reason You bring children

across our paths is to teach

us important lessons.

It wasn't long ago that I heard

a small child thanking You for many things.

"And thank You for the lightning bugs,"

he said. What a simple reminder

that there's nothing too insignificant

for which to offer thanks.

Purity

The name of Jesus. . .awakened similar emotions
in the hearts of all the converts, and
called immediately into action every feeling
of moral loveliness, and every desire of dutiful
obedience, which constitute Christian purity.

JOHN STRACHAN

Think on Pure Things

There's just not much in today's society

that encourages purity,

but Your Word certainly demonstrates

the importance of focusing our attention

upon things that are pure.

From experience, I have learned that life

is more satisfying when it's geared

toward pleasing You rather than the flesh,

and I thank You for these lessons.

Winter Snow

What a beautiful illustration of purity
You've given us in a blanket
of fresh-fallen snow.
It's the kind of purity
You want for my life,
and it's the cleanliness
that only You can give.
I am so grateful for Your saving blood
that washed my life white as snow.

Cleansing Flames

You wanted to use me, Father,

but You knew there were areas

in my heart that first needed cleansing.

You knew the only way to accomplish

this would be to send purifying flames.

The testing fires were painful sometimes,

but I'm glad You sent them.

It felt good to be washed

and worthy of service.

True Purity

Father, please show me if the life

I live is truly pure in Your sight.

In my pride, I'm afraid I raise myself

to greater heights than I ought to

where cleanliness is involved.

But I want to see myself through Your eyes.

I want to measure up to Your standards.

Please purify my attitude, Lord.

Cleanse My Lips

You had a job for Moses,

but he said he couldn't speak.

Isaiah, on the other hand, was willing.

You simply had to cleanse his lips

so that the words You gave him

would come forth purely.

You've given me a message to share, too.

I just pray that You would touch

my mouth with Your coals.

Relationships

*The best relationship is the one in which your love
for each other exceeds your need for each other.*

UNKNOWN

～∞～

People in My Life

I know that You've brought people

into my life for many different reasons,

but I have to admit that sometimes

I'd like to take my dog

and move to my own island.

It's hard to please people,

and it's easy to upset them.

Neither situation is pleasant for me.

Lord, please help me do

my best in each relationship.

The Best Relationship

Dear Jesus, I've known many people in my life.

I've enjoyed many good relationships

and tried to avoid the bad.

One thing is certain, though.

My relationship with You

is the most important.

I'm so glad You have time for me and that

You want me to fellowship with You.

I couldn't ask for a better friend.

Harmful Relationships

Lord, I generally think of relationships

as being between people,

and I fail to remember that

my relationship to things can seriously

affect how I react to people.

For instance, sometimes I get so involved

in a television show that I fail

to give needed attention to my family.

Forgive me, Father.

Be in charge of my relationships.

Good Relationships

Thank You, Lord, for giving me

a good relationship with

my husband and children.

So many people struggle

with unhappy homes,

and it's only Your grace

that protects me from that.

I ask that You'd keep Your hand

on our home and give others

happy lives, as well.

Expert Advice

I am amazed at the wisdom
that King Solomon extended
to his son in the Proverbs, Lord.
I guess he would have had expert
knowledge concerning relationships,
though, since he'd been
involved in so many.
I'm glad he talks about both
the good and the bad, too.
It gives me courage to choose
good companions.

Rest

Rest is not idleness, and to lie sometimes on
the grass under the trees on a summer's day,
listening to the murmur of water,
or watching the clouds float across the sky,
is by no means a waste of time.

JOHN LUBBOCK

Finding Time to Rest

I find it difficult to even

sit down to a meal, Father.

Resting seems like such

a far-fetched notion.

I know You want me to find time to rest

and spend time with You,

but I'm on the go constantly,

and I still don't get everything done.

Please help me, Lord,

to make resting a priority.

Resting on the Porch Swing

In my mind resting usually
translates into sleep,
but as I sit here on the porch swing,
gliding slowly back and forth, and
thinking about nothing in particular,
I am reminded that relaxing
takes on many forms.
I feel blessed indeed that
rest is part of Your plan.

Balancing Work and Rest

I had to chuckle as I read the verse that says,

"Give not sleep to thine eyes"

(Proverbs 6:4).

I guess I don't have much

trouble obeying that!

I have more difficulty with

"Come. . .apart. . .and rest a while"

(Mark 6:31).

I think I'm getting the picture, though.

Please help me learn to

balance work and rest.

A Day of Rest

You established a day of rest following

Your completion of creation, God.

Although You expect us to

spend time with You daily,

You knew how much we would need a day

to retreat from our normal activities,

to fellowship with other believers,

and to focus primarily on You.

Help me never take this day

of rest for granted.

Entering God's Rest

Dear Jesus, in this world,

we will never experience true rest,

but You've offered this tantalizing

refreshment to anyone who will enter it. Yet

so many reject this repose You offer.

It's a refusal I can't fathom, Lord.

Show them what they are missing.

Draw them into Your rest today.

Salvation

No man can fail of the benefits
of Christ's salvation,
but through an unwillingness to have it.

WILLIAM LAW

The Greatest Salvation

Salvation is something we all long for

in one way or another, Father,

and the salvation You've provided

far surpasses anything that

could be presented by mankind.

You've rescued me from the depths of sin

and given me new life in Christ,

and I will ever praise You!

Salvation of Loved Ones

There are many people in my family

who have not accepted Your gift

of salvation, dear Jesus.

My most heartfelt prayer for each

of them is that they will trust You.

Draw each of them into Your embrace.

I pray that each would receive You as Savior.

Let the Children Come

You said that accepting You
requires childlike faith, dear Jesus.
Yet so often we fail to take
the young ones seriously.
We think they're too young to understand,
but You said to let them come.
Give us wisdom when dealing
with the little ones,
and help us encourage them
to accept You, as well.

Stand Still, and See
the Salvation of the Lord

We are such a frenetic lot, dear God,

but when we get all worked up,

You say, "Stand still."

You offer complete salvation

but only when we take the time

to see from where our deliverance comes.

Help us slow down and witness

the greatest of miracles.

Good Enough?

When I stand before
the Great White Throne,
won't it be enough that I was a good person?
Won't it matter that
I went to church and tithed?
I even taught Sunday school.
Will You really say, "Depart from me"
(Matthew 25:41)?
Is that what Your Word means by,
"Not by works of righteousness. . .
but according to his mercy he saved us"
(Titus 3:5)?

Self-Esteem

Nothing profits more than self-esteem,
grounded on what is just and right.

JOHN MILTON

Christlikeness

There's such a fine line between

self-esteem and arrogance.

Sometimes I have trouble

distinguishing between the two. Father,

You created me in Your image.

For that I am thankful,

but I need to remember that I'm not perfect.

Help me not to be proud

but to daily strive to be more like You.

Building Self-Esteem

I remember when I was little
how embarrassing it was to be teased
about my nerdy assortment of clothing.
And it hurt when the
"big kids" picked on me,
but You also brought people into my life
who uplifted and encouraged me.
What a blessing they were!
Lord, let me build another
person's self-esteem.

Affecting Others

Lately I've been feeling a little low, Father.

I'm not meeting those expectations

I have of myself, and I've been

dragging myself down.

Unfortunately, my lack of self-esteem

is pulling others down, too.

I don't want to do that.

I want to give my frustrations to You

and let You work through me.

Special to the Father

How can I doubt my worth
in Your eyes, Father?
You know the number of hairs on my head.
You created me, and You said
that Your creation is very good.
When I'm tempted to get down on myself,
remind me that I am special to You,
and there's no one just like me.

Still Working on Me

Dear God, I'm a far cry from perfect,

but I'm confident in the knowledge

that You love me just as I am.

You are the One who

has begun a work in me,

and You will be faithful

to complete what has been started.

What a thrill to know that You'll

make me what You want me to be.

Service

It is distinctive of the Christian life,
that while it grows more conscientious,
it also grows less and less a task of duty
and more and more a service of delight.

Newman Smyth

Lessons from Feet

Jesus, I read the story about how
You washed Your disciples' feet, and I
thought about how unpleasant that might
have been. Were You thinking that those
same feet would carry Your gospel to
the world? They were no longer appalling,
but beautiful. I will wash feet if You
call me to, or I'll carry Your message.

Saved to Serve

I'm not sure how many times
I've heard the saying
"God saved me to serve, not to sit."
There are so many ways I can
be involved in Christian service.
What I need most is a willing heart.
Help me never to lose sight of the fact
that servanthood is beautiful in
Your sight and a blessing to others.

It's All Important

You know, when I was little,

I had chores to do.

I didn't want to do them because

they didn't seem important.

I wanted to do meaningful work.

Now I find myself with

the same attitude at times.

You show me a job that needs to be done,

but I ignore it because

I want something more challenging.

Forgive me, Lord.

In Your eyes it's all important.

A Servant's Heart

The irony in Your Word

makes me smile, Lord.

When You speak of greatness,

it's in connection with servanthood.

It's so contrary to human nature,

but when I think about it,

it really does make sense.

That still doesn't make it easy, though.

Please give me a servant's heart.

Martha's Trap

Lord, I want to be a servant,

but I want it to be done Your way.

Please don't let me get caught in Martha's

trap of meeting only the physical needs.

Although those elements are important,

they don't reach the whole person.

Let me be a blessing in the spiritual

and emotional areas, too.

Stress

The little troubles and worries of life
may be as stumbling blocks in our way,
or we may make them stepping-stones
to a nobler character and to heaven.

HENRY WARD BEECHER

The Popularity of Stress

Stress seems so overrated these days,

doesn't it, Lord?

Every time I turn around

someone is telling me how stressed they are.

And I do the same thing.

I guess it's popular to be stressed.

Popular maybe—but not good.

Please take my stress and turn it into energy

that is used for Your glory.

A Load of Stress

Deadlines, sports schedules,

unexpected overnight company—

I'm about to pull out my hair!

I know we all have our share of stress,

but didn't I get an extra load this week, Father?

I'm not sure what the purpose of it is,

but I know there's a reason.

Lord, give me patience through the ordeal,

and let me please You.

One Step at a Time

It's the end of another day, Father.
I didn't accomplish enough,
and tomorrow looms nearby
with all of its expectations.
I want to rejoice in the days You give me,
but honestly it's been a chore merely to
put one foot in front of the other.
The stress of the load weighs me down.
Please grant me the strength
to take one step at a time.

Stress and Vulnerability

Dear God, I've discovered that
during these times of stress I seem
more vulnerable to temptation.
I need You even more
during this trying hour.
I must lean on You and on the
godly friends You've provided.
Help me to focus on the goal,
and keep me from faltering.

I Failed to Trust You

Forgive me, Father.

Time and again I've been so stressed

that I wanted to give up on life.

I tried so hard to get through each day,

but I never bothered to give

my worries to You.

I've fought through each task

and brought grief to others

by trying to struggle alone,

but from now on,

I'm casting my cares on You!

True Beauty

Favour is deceitful, and beauty is vain:
but a woman that feareth the LORD,
she shall be praised.

PROVERBS 31:30

Lessons from a Child

I saw the prettiest child at the park today,

Father. Her beautiful smile reached her eyes.

I think it must have reached her heart, too,

because I also saw this little girl go right up

and play with a child who had a disability,

and whom other kids were teasing.

Lord, thank You for showing me

what inner beauty is.

The Beauty of Christ

You know, Lord,

I spend a lot of time each morning

trying to look physically attractive.

That doesn't do much for my soul, though.

Sure, I feel better when I look nice,

but I know if people saw Your beauty in me,

that would bring more joy.

Draw me close, and make this a reality.

In Spite of the Grime

This afternoon I asked my husband
to help me with a task
that was neither clean nor fun.
When we'd completed the chore,
we were both filthy.
But at that moment
I saw a beautiful person.
He had other plans,
but because I needed help,
he gave willingly.
That's beautiful!

Incorruptible Beauty

I was glancing through a magazine today,
and there were so many tips
on being beautiful.
As I looked at the models,
I thought about how few people
really look like that.
And I realized something like a car crash
could change it all instantly.
Inner beauty isn't like that, is it, Father?
It's from You, and it's incorruptible.

Already Beautiful

Yesterday I heard a little boy ask his mother

why she was purchasing cosmetics.

"To help me look better," was her reply.

"But you're beautiful,"

the boy said with conviction.

The mother smiled brightly

and gave the child a hug.

As he returned the embrace,

the love between them was unmistakable.

Lord, at that moment I knew—

she was beautiful!

Wisdom

Pure wisdom always directs itself toward God;
the purest wisdom is knowledge of God.

Lew Wallace

∞∞∞

God's Wisdom

I'm so forgetful!

God, I know how many times You've

admonished me to seek Your wisdom,

yet over and over I try to

do things on my own.

You'd think I would learn

after so many mistakes,

but I guess I'm too proud.

I don't want to continue like this.

I want Your wisdom so that

I can live life as You intended.

Making Decisions

I'm facing a situation right now,
and I'm not quite sure
how to handle it, Father.
I'm coming to You because
I truly lack wisdom,
but I need to know how
to make the right decision.
Thank You for promising that
You will guide me.

God's Book of Wisdom

There are so many "how-to" books

available today, Lord,

and they all promise to increase

my knowledge in some area.

But not one of them gives

any hope for added wisdom.

Only Your Word offers that.

Thank You for providing the means

to know You more fully

and to live life more abundantly.

Solomon's Choice

You gave Solomon an opportunity

to ask of You any gift he desired,

and he asked for wisdom.

Thus he received many more blessings.

I'd like to think I would

have asked the same,

but I don't know if I would have.

Please make me more mature so

I'll ask for things that really matter.

Having Wisdom and Applying It

Lord, You've given me a wealth
of wisdom right there in Your Word,
but knowing what's there and acting
upon it are two entirely different things.
Sometimes my behavior is still so foolish.
Forgive me, Lord.
Help me not to ignore the direction
You've given me.
Help me to walk wisely.

Work

Opportunity is missed by most people because it comes dressed in overalls and looks like work.

THOMAS EDISON

Prioritizing

Father, I really have a lot to do,

and I'm not very good at multitasking.

I need Your help each day as I organize

the chores that need to be done.

Show me how to prioritize my workload

so that I can get things done in the

most efficient manner, and let

my work be pleasing in Your sight.

Enjoyable Work

I'm blessed to have a job I enjoy, Lord.

So many people aren't able to say the same,

and many of them probably

have good reason to dislike their work.

Thank You for opening this door

of opportunity for me.

You've met my needs in a wonderful way.

Difficult Coworkers

I don't know how much longer

I can take this.

Father, when I accepted this job

I really thought I was getting

into a good situation,

but the people I work with are so fake.

Everyone is in it for self-gratification—

not for the company or those we serve.

I'm so tired of it.

Please help me through this difficult time.

Workaholic

Is this really healthy, Lord?

The more I work,

the more I find that needs to be done.

It seems I'm only content when I'm busy,

but even though accomplishments

are exciting, I seem to be

missing out on simple pleasures.

I really want to learn

to enjoy stopping to smell the roses.

Menial Tasks

Do You ever wish we'd eliminate

the phrase "menial task"

from our vocabulary, Father?

I know that all work is important

to You and that the attitude

I have when performing each duty

holds even greater weight.

Help me to remember

that even the small jobs

have significance in light

of the bigger picture.

About the Author

Rachel Quillin is the author of several gift books and coauthor of the devotional prayer book *Prayers & Promises for Mothers*. She makes her home in eastern Ohio with her husband Eric and their children.

Prayer Notes

Prayer Notes

Prayer Notes

Prayer Notes

Prayer Notes

Prayer Notes

Prayer Notes

Prayer Notes

Prayer Notes

Prayer Notes

Prayer Notes

Prayer Notes

Prayer Notes

Prayer Notes

Prayer Notes

Prayer Notes

Prayer Notes